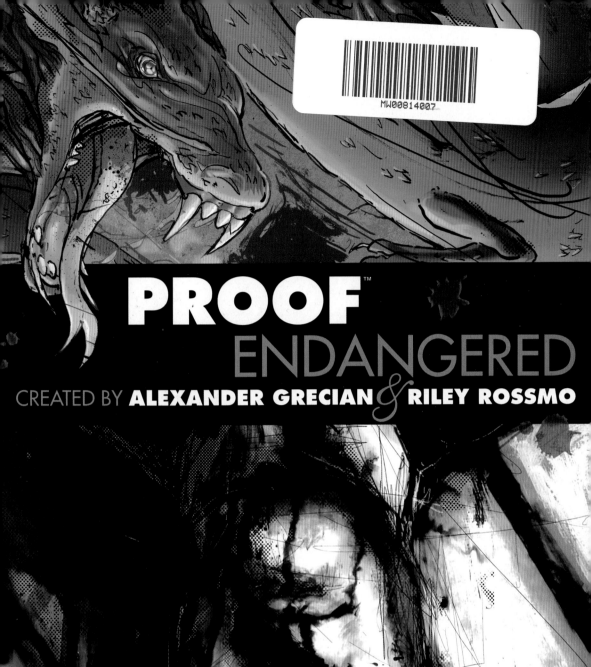

PROOF™
ENDANGERED

CREATED BY **ALEXANDER GRECIAN** & **RILEY ROSSMO**

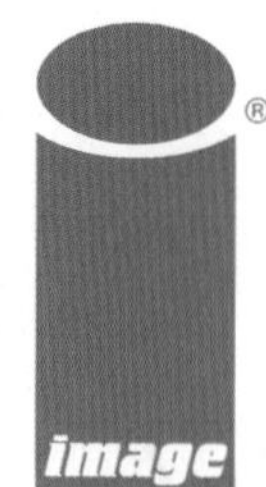

IMAGE COMICS, INC.

ROBERT KIRKMAN chief operating officer ERIK LARSEN chief financial officer TODD McFARLANE president
MARK SILVESTRI chief executive officer JIM VALENTINO vice-president

ERIC STEPHENSON publisher TODD MARTINEZ sales & licensing coordinator SARAH deLAINE pr & marketing coordinator
BRANWYN BIGGLESTONE accounts manager EMILY MILLER administrative assistant JAMIE PARRERO marketing assistant
KEVIN YUEN digital rights coordinator TYLER SHAINLINE production manager DREW GILL art director JONATHAN CHAN sr production artist
MONICA GARCIA production artist VINCENT KUKUA production artist JANA COOK production artist

www.imagecomics.com

PROOF.VOL. 6: ENDANGERED
ISBN: 978-1-60706-391-9
First Printing

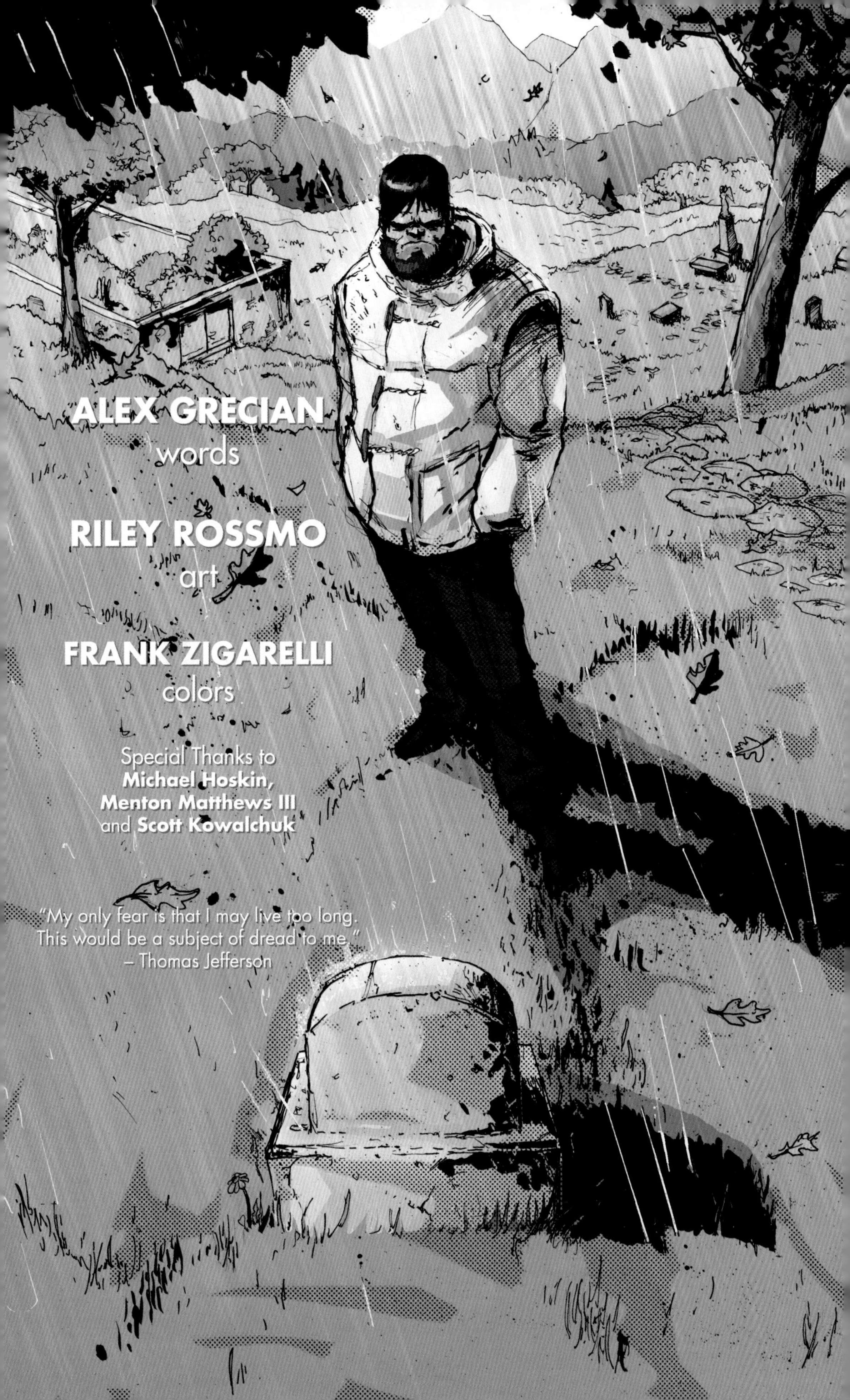
ALEX GRECIAN
words
RILEY ROSSMO
art
FRANK ZIGARELLI
colors
Special Thanks to
Michael Hoskin,
Menton Matthews III
and Scott Kowalchuk
"My only fear is that I may live too long.
This would be a subject of dread to me."
– Thomas Jefferson

LITTLE TOKYO

SUSHIMI

茶酒

行

EXOTIC FOOD

YESTERDAY

GET DOWN SIR.

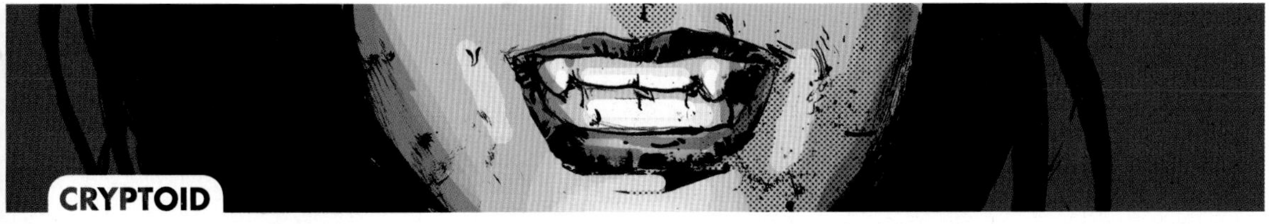

CRYPTOID

The chupacabra is rarely seen in its natural form. It is a vicious predator with no known natural enemies. It tends to prey on cattle, picking off the weakest member of a herd, then using the cow's skin and a variety of camouflage abilities to help it infiltrate the herd, where it is able to feed from within. It is assumed that some chupacabras have used human skins to walk among us undetected.

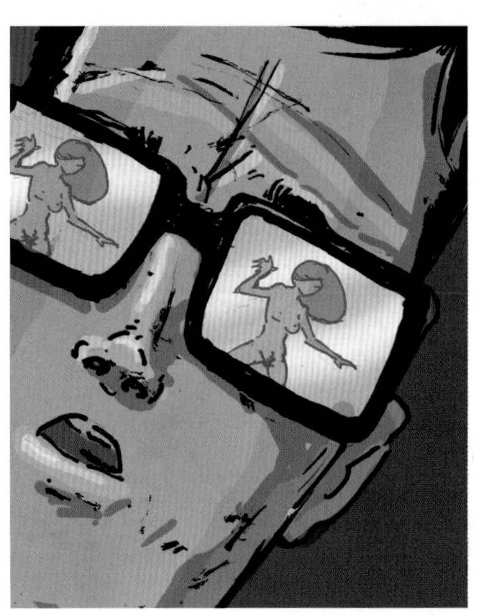

IS IT DONE?
YES, SIR.

GOOD. LET'S FINISH THIS AND GET OUT OF HERE.

EARLY THIS MORNING

UNIFORMS FOUND A PILE OF MEAT AND BONES IN THE ALLEY OUT BACK. LOOKS HUMAN.

YES, THIS HAS BEEN THE WORK OF MINE KIND.

"No human thing is of serious importance." – Plato

WE FOUND THIS IN THE KITCHEN. IT'S JUST--
AN EMPTY SKIN.
THE CHUPACABRA'S CHANGED SKINS AND MOVED ON.

ITS SCENT IS IN THE AIR HERE AND THIS IS NOT ANYONE I KNOW.
SO WE GOT A STRANGE CHUPACABRA RUNNIN' AROUND HOLLOWIN' FOLKS OUT.

YOU KEEP SNIFFIN' AROUND. I GOT A CALL TO MAKE.

YOU'RE KIDDING ME.
NO, I APPRECIATE THE CALL. PLEASE KEEP US IN THE LOOP.

TIME TO GET UP, SLEEPYHEAD. THINGS ARE HAPPENING.
THAT WAS BELINDA. SHE'S RIGHT HERE IN LITTLE TOKYO AND SOMETHING'S GOING ON.
GIMME FIVE MORE MINUTES?

THERE'S A CHUPACABRA HERE SOMEWHERE.

THAT CAN'T BE A COINCIDENCE. CALL THE OTHERS.

ALREADY ON IT.
GOOD. I'LL GET US PACKED. YOU FIND OUT WHERE THE BIG MAN IS.

WHAT DO YOU THINK?
DON' DRINK!

WHAT DO I THINK?
I THINK YOU OWE ME.

JUST LOOK AT THIS, WILL YOU? IT'S A SASQUATCH FINGER.
DO YOU THINK YOU CAN TELL ME WHERE IT CAME FROM?

WHY DON'T YOU LOOK AT THAT CONTRACT YOU SIGNED? YOU KNOW WHERE *IT* CAME FROM, RIGHT?
WHY AIN'T YOU DEAD ALREADY?

WHAT'S HE TALKING ABOUT?
IT'S COMPLICATED.
TRY ME.

A COUPLE OF GENERATIONS BACK, I NEEDED SOME HELP AND I PROMISED THE SONG FAMILY SOMETHING IN RETURN. THEY ASKED FOR MY REMAINS. THEY ASKED TO BE ALLOWED TO DISPLAY MY BODY AFTER I DIED.
I SOLD THEM MY DEAD BODY IN ADVANCE.
NONE OF US EXPECTED ME TO LIVE SO LONG.

YOU DIDN'T TELL NOBODY YOU WERE FUCKING IMMORTAL.
MY GREAT GRANDFATHER RISKED EVERYTHING FOR YOU AND GOT NOTHING IN RETURN.
I DON'T THINK I *AM* IMMORTAL HOW WAS I SUPPOSED TO KNOW HOW LONG I'D LIVE?
I WASN'T TRYING TO CHEAT ANYONE.
SO, WHAT THEN? THIS IN HERE'S SUPPOSED TO BE A BIGFOOT FINGER?
YOU FIGURE I'LL FIND OUT WHOSE ARM IT BELONGS TO AND IN EXCHANGE FOR THAT I GET MORE OF THE SAME NOTHING YOU ALWAYS GIVE MY FAMILY?
WHAT DO YOU WANT THEN?
WHAT CAN I GIVE YOU IN RETURN FOR YOUR HELP?
NO, WAIT. THIS IS RIDICULOUS. YOU CAN'T SELL SOMEONE YOUR BODY. I MEAN, YOU CAN, BUT THAT MAKES YOU--
AT THE TIME I DIDN'T HAVE ANYTHING ELSE TO BARTER WITH. BUT I HAVE MONEY NOW.
I DON'T NEED MONEY. I GOT MONEY.
SNAP
I WANT WHAT I'M OWED.
AND I WANT IT NOW.

OH, RIVER...

CRASH

CRASH

IF ANYBODY GETS TO KILL PROOF, IT'S GOING TO BE ME.
EEEE!
"DID YOU HEAR SOMETHING?"

"MORE LIKE I *FELT* IT. EARTHQUAKE, MAYBE."
"GREAT. I FORGOT ABOUT EARTHQUAKES."

DO YOU MISS SEATTLE?
NOT MUCH. THAT CHAPTER OF MY LIFE FELT LIKE IT WAS DRAWING TO A CLOSE.
HOW 'BOUT YOU?

WHAT DO YOU THINK OF THIS?
TRY IT ON. ARE YOU DODGING MY QUESTION?
I THINK ELVIS WOULD LIKE IT.

DO I MISS SEATTLE?
I DON'T KNOW. I LIKED IT THERE, BUT IT'S NOT LIKE I LIVED THERE A LONG TIME.
WHAT I LIKED MOST ABOUT IT WAS SOME OF THE PEOPLE. AND MOST OF THE PEOPLE I LIKED ARE HERE WITH US NOW.

YOU THINK ELVIS WILL LIKE THE GUN BULGE THERE?
OH, WHOOPS. MAYBE NOT.

MAYBE I SHOULD GET A SWORD.

YOU **HAVE** TO HAVE A WEAPON?
YOU'VE BEEN AROUND PROOF LONG ENOUGH. WOULD YOU GO UNARMED?
I **DO** GO UNARMED.

I THINK I SAW SWORDS BACK HERE SOMEWHERE.
YOU'RE SERIOUS?

VOILA!
I REALLY THOUGHT YOU WERE KIDDING. THEY ACTUALLY HAVE SWORDS!

KRAK
WHAT WAS THAT?

YOU LADIES HAVE NO WORRY. ONLY LITTLE EARTHQUAKE. VERY SMALL. NO HARM. I WILL CHECK THE BREAKER AND BE RIGHT BACK.
YOU SHOP, SHOP. IT IS FUN TO SHOP IN THE DARK.

HEY, IT'S FUN TO SHOP IN THE DARK.
WHO KNEW?
HE PROBABLY DOES THIS HIMSELF SO HE CAN SELL THE UGLIEST STUFF WHEN YOU CAN'T SEE IT.
SURE, I WAS ALREADY PLANNING TO JUST RANDOMLY GRAB--

WHO ARE YOU? TAKE THAT OFF!
NO, DON'T--
ARRRGGH!

MISTER LEE? MISTER LEE, ARE YOU OKAY?

HERE, TAKE THIS. BE CAREFUL AND DON'T SHOOT ME.
CALL FOR HELP.
WHAT ARE YOU GOING TO DO?

I'M GONNA GO CHECK ON MISTER LEE.

OH, SHIT.
Hello, Ginger.

The federal government owns more than thirty percent of the total land area of Washington state. The overall majority of land owned by the government is concentrated in the most heavily-forested western third of the country, which is, coincidentally, where Bigfoot is most often sighted.

THE LODGE

DING

THEY'RE HERE ALREADY?
SUPPOSED TO BE HERE TOMORROW, DAMNIT.

YOU READY FOR THIS? GONNA BE A BIG STEP DOWN FOR YOU.
NOT NECESSARILY. THESE PEOPLE DON'T KNOW ANYTHING ABOUT THIS PLACE.
IT WOULD MAKE SENSE FOR THEM TO KEEP ME ON.
MIGHT MAKE SENSE, BUT THIS IS THE GOVERNMENT WE'RE TALKING ABOUT.

NO TELLING WHAT THEY'RE GONNA DECIDE TO DO AROUND HERE.

I'LL GO BRING 'EM BACK UP HERE. YOU GET YOURSELF READY TO DEAL WITH THIS.

WELCOME TO THE LODGE, SIR.
I'D BE HAPPY TO SHOW YOU THE GROUNDS, SENATOR, AND EXPLAIN WHAT GOES ON HERE.

THAT WON'T BE NECESSAR SOLDIER

IN FACT, YOU'RE RELIEVED OF DUTY.
I'LL BE TAKING OVER.
YOU HAVE TWENTY-FOUR HOURS TO VACATE THIS PROPERTY.

1814
POPLAR FOREST, VIRGINIA,
THE HOME OF THOMAS JEFFERSON

DAMN!

RARRRGGH!

I'M NOT A MONKEY.
SILLY MONKEY.
I KNOW THAT, DUMMIE.
THESE CLOTHES ARE UNCOMFORTABLE AND I DON'T LIKE THEM.
WELL, THAT'S NO REASON TO FLING THEM ABOUT THE ROOM.
YOU CAN'T RUN AROUND THE HOUSE WEARING A LOINCLOTH ALL YOUR LIFE.
WHY NOT?
YOU KNOW PERFECTLY WELL WHY NOT.

THERE. HOW'S THAT?
IT'S GOOD. THANK YOU, CORDELIA.
IF YOU DON'T WANT TO LIVE WITH US AND WEAR OUR CLOTHES, YOU CAN ALWAYS GO BACK TO YOUR REAL FAMILY, YOU KNOW.
BUT IT WOULD BREAK GRANDPA'S HEART.
AND IT WOULD MAKE ME VERY SAD TOO.
ARE YOU COMING TO DINNER?
I'LL BE THERE IN A MOMENT.

LITTLE TOKYO
TODAY
POPPOP

I HAVE A MESSAGE FROM YOUR BROTHER, PROOF.
HE'S UPSET THAT YOU NEVER VISIT.

WHOA!
WHAT BROTHER? WHAT DO YOU KNOW ABOUT MY FAMILY?

OH, YOU KNOW... HE'S A BIG GUY? WHITE FUR? ABANDONMENT ISSUES?

UFF
YOU'RE TALKING ABOUT GILGAMESH?
YOU'RE HERE BECAUSE OF THE DAMN YETI?

HE HASN'T CALLED HIMSELF GILGAMESH IN YEARS.
HE GOES BY THE NAME MI-CHEN-PO NOW.
AND DON'T TELL HIM, BUT I HAVE MY OWN AGENDA...

PROBLEMS WITH MY OWN BROTHER.

HELLO, RIVER. I'M HERE TO KILL YOU.

CRYPTOID

The **Mongolian Death Worm** is generally only seen when the ground warms up in June and July. It spurts a green acidic foam that dissolves its prey and it apparently generates a strong electrical field. Eyewitnesses claim to have seen a death worm kill a visiting geologist by simply touching an iron rod that the man was holding.

ENOUGH!
I'VE HAD ENOUGH!

GILGAMESH OR MI-CHEN-PO OR WHATEVER HE WANTS TO CALL HIMSELF...
HE WAS NEVER MY BROTHER. HE'S A PUNK WITH DELUSIONS OF GRANDEUR.
HE'S THE EXACT OPPOSITE OF EVERYTHING I AM.

WHERE IS HE? WHY ARE YOU DEALING WITH HIM?

TELL ME!
IT DOESN'T MATTER WHAT I TELL YOU. THERE'S NOTHING YOU CAN DO. YOUR BROTHER PLANNED EVERY-THING AND IT'S TOO LATE.
"PLANNED" WHAT? WHAT THE HELL ARE YOU TALKING ABOUT?

RIGHT NOW, WHILE YOU WASTE TIME WITH ME, PO'S OTHER AGENT IS KILLING EVERYBODY YOU EVER CARED ABOUT.

KILLING--?
BELLA!
GINGER!

THE LODGE

WAIT! NO, WHAT ARE YOU DOING?
ISN'T IT OBVIOUS? I AM ADDING TO YOUR COLLECTION OF CREATURES.

YOU CAN'T JUST INDISCRIMINATELY JAM ANIMALS IN HERE. THE HABITAT IS A DELICATE ECOSYSTEM.

I RECOGNIZE-- THESE ARE THE BLUE MEN OF THE MINCH. WHERE DID YOU GET THEM?
FROM THE MINCH, OF COURSE. IT'S IN SCOTLAND.
I KNOW WHERE THEY COME FROM. I'VE BEEN SEARCHING FOR THEM FOR YEARS. I'M ASKING... HOW DID YOU ACQUIRE THEM?

MY SPONSOR HAS QUITE A COLLECTION. HE'S DONATED THESE SPECIMENS.

I WAS TOLD THERE WERE FAIRIES HERE. WHERE ARE THEY?
YOUR SPONSOR? WHO'S YOUR SPONSOR? WHAT DO YOU MEAN?
WHAT DO YOU--?

WAIT. THAT'S ODD. I DON'T THINK I'VE SEEN A FAIRY IN DAYS. MAYBE WEEKS.
THEY *WERE* ALL OVER THE PLACE.

GOOD. I DISLIKE FAIRIES. BUT IF THEY'VE DISAPPEARED, THE BLUE MEN MAY NOT BE NECESSARY AFTER ALL.
OPEN IT UP.
WHAT ARE YOU DOING HERE? I DON'T UNDERSTAND WHAT'S GOING ON.

NO MORE. DON'T DO ANYTHING ELSE. I'M CALLING WASHINGTON.
GO AHEAD AND BRING THEM OUT. I HAVE THE AUTHORITY HERE.

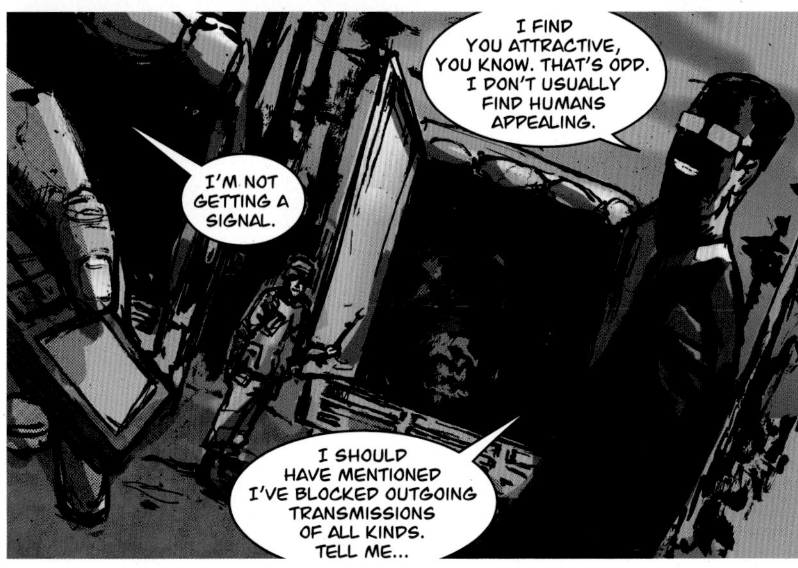
I'M NOT GETTING A SIGNAL.
I FIND YOU ATTRACTIVE, YOU KNOW. THAT'S ODD. I DON'T USUALLY FIND HUMANS APPEALING.
I SHOULD HAVE MENTIONED I'VE BLOCKED OUTGOING TRANSMISSIONS OF ALL KINDS. TELL ME...

YOU'RE NOT HUMAN AT ALL, ARE YOU?
WHO ARE YOU?

I'VE SEEN MONSTERS, ASSHOLE AND YOU'RE NO MONSTER. YOU'RE JUST SOME DOUCHEBAG IN A COSTUME.

Don't you know me, Ginger?

I'm your death!

"Life being what it is, one dreams of revenge." – Paul Gauguin

Oh, wait... I did!
And look what I got to replace it!

THUNK

Hold on. I'm stuck!

HURK

YOU OKAY?
WOOF!

I THINK SO. THANKS.
WHAT TOOK YOU SO LONG?
I HAD TO FIND SOMETHING TO HIT HIM WITH. IT'S ALL PILLOWS HERE.

HE ACTED LIKE HE KNEW YOU.
I THINK HE'S AN EX-BOYFRIEND.
MUST'VE BEEN ONE HELL OF A BREAK-UP.

POOR MISTER LEE.
"POOR MISTER LEE" NOTHING.
EEP!

GET ME DOWN FROM HERE.
UM... WE THOUGHT YOU WERE DEAD.
CUT ME DOWN NOW!

HOLD STILL.
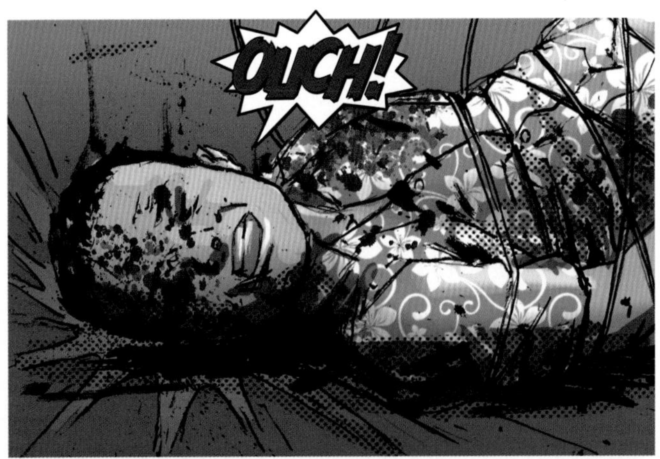
OUCH!

MY HEAD HURTS.
HOLD STILL. LET ME GET THIS OFF YOU.

YOU LADIES CALL THE POLICE YET? CALL THE POLICE RIGHT NOW.
WE WILL, BUT YOU NEED TO LET ME LOOK AT YOUR WOUNDS.
GIVE ME THAT ROPE SO I CAN SECURE THIS--

OH, YOU'RE KIDDING ME.
HE'S GONE?

TAKE CARE OF MISTER LEE AND CALL IT IN. I'M GONNA FIND THIS SCOOBY-DOO VILLAIN.

IF THIS IS SUCH A BAD GUY, HOW COME YOU NEVER TOLD ME ABOUT HIM?
THE LODGE

IF I'D TOLD YOU ABOUT HIM, YOU WOULD'VE HAD TO DO SOMETHING.
LIKE WHAT?
I DON'T KNOW, BUT I DIDN'T WANT TO PUT YOU IN A DIFFICULT POSITION.

BUT YOU DON'T EVEN KNOW WHAT KIND OF POSITION YOU'D BE PUTTING ME IN.
NOT EXACTLY. BUT I IMAGINE IT WOULD HAVE MORALLY COMPROMISED YOU.
WHAT EXACTLY DID YOU DO TO THIS GUY, WAYNE?

I BELIEVE I MAY QUALIFY AS A WAR CRIMINAL.

YOU SAID THIS WAS WHERE THE FAIRIES SWARM?
USED TO BE.
THEN WHERE ARE THEY?

THAT'S THE BIG QUESTION, ISN'T IT?
I THOUGHT I WAS BEING CLEVER. WE KEPT THE MOST DANGEROUS HUMAN ALIVE IN A PLACE WHERE THE MOST DANGEROUS CREATURES WOULD KEEP HIM TRAPPED.
BUT IF THE FAIRIES ARE GONE, THAT MEANS THERE'S NOTHING KEEPING HIM HERE ANYMORE.

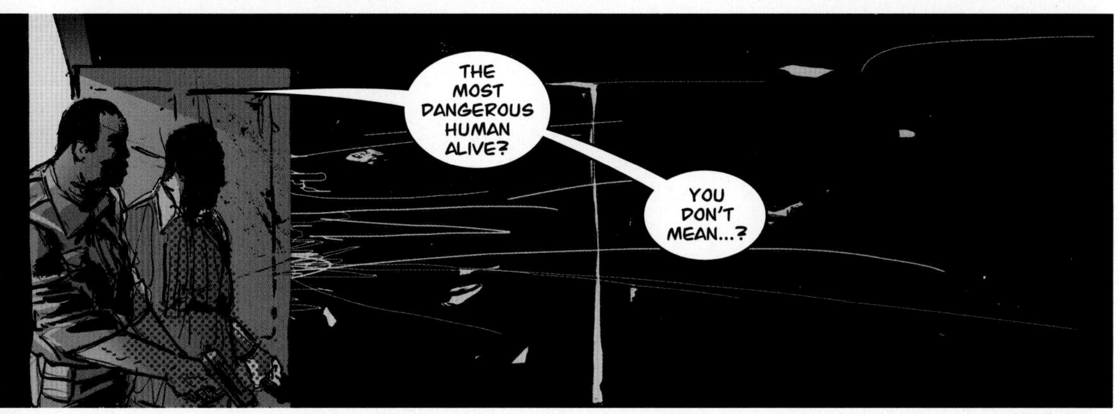
THE MOST DANGEROUS HUMAN ALIVE?
YOU DON'T MEAN...?

I THINK HE MEANS ME.

I'M FLATTERED.
THANK YOU FOR ALL THE FAIRIES, WAYNE.
THEY WERE DELICIOUS.

SHE'S NOT PICKING UP.
WHERE ARE THEY?
WHAT'S THAT SOUND? THAT RUMBLING?

I DON'T KNOW WHERE THEY ARE. THEY'RE JUST SHOPPING.
THERE'S LIKE A ZILLION STORES HERE. WHAT DO WE DO, SHOUT THEIR NAMES AND HOPE THEY HEAR US?

WAIT. GIVE ME A MINUTE. MAYBE I CAN ISOLATE BELLA'S PERFUME.

NO TIME FOR THAT!
YOU'VE GOT YOUR OWN PROBLEMS TO DEAL WITH, BROTHER...
TCHEN

I'VE ASKED MY FRIEND TO KILL YOUR FRIENDS!

I DON'T KNOW WHAT YOU'RE DOING HERE, MARC, BUT I KNOW IT'S YOU IN THAT COSTUME.

COME OUT AND LET'S TALK. IT'S NOT TOO LATE.

I REALLY DON'T WANT TO HURT YOU.

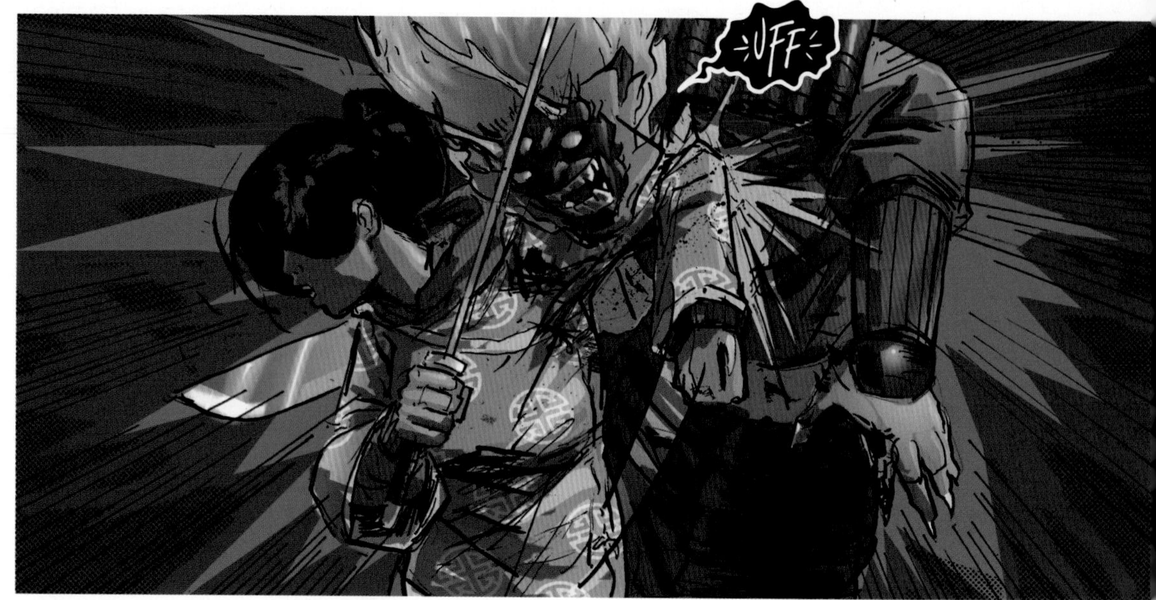
UFF

HEY, I GUESS I WAS WRONG...

I KINDA DID WANT TO HURT YOU.

CRASH

WHAT THE HELL IS THIS ALL ABOUT, HUH?

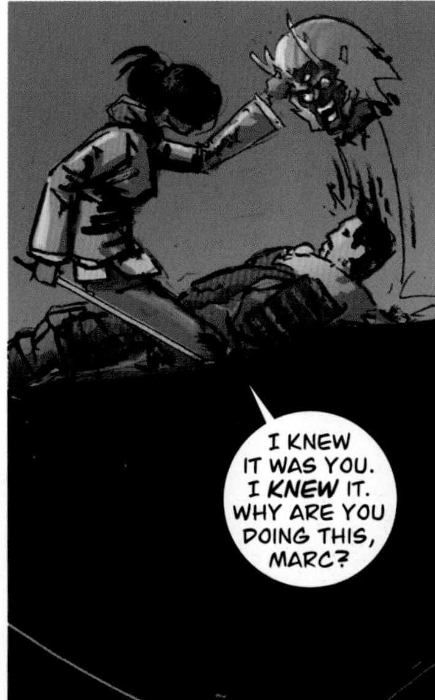
I KNEW IT WAS YOU. I **KNEW** IT. WHY ARE YOU DOING THIS, MARC?

BABY, DO YOU REMEMBER HOW MUCH I LOVED YOU?

GAHH!
WELL, THAT'S HOW MUCH I HATE YOU NOW!

AND I AIN'T ALONE. MY NEW BOSS HAS A MESSAGE FOR YOU...

HEY, RUBE.

I STILL LOVE--

HURK

GINGER?

GINGER, ARE YOU OKAY?
CAN YOU ANSWER? ARE YOU HURT?

WHOEVER'S IN HERE WITH US, YOU SHOULD KNOW THAT I HAVE A GUN.

AND I'VE CALLED THE POLICE SO YOU SHOULD LEAVE WHILE YOU STILL CAN.

GINGER WHERE ARE YOU?
WHAT DO YOU MEAN SHE'S "GONE?"

...WE LEFT AUTUMN AND HER BROTHER RIGHT THERE.

YEAH, I CAN SEE WHERE YOU HAD 'EM TIED UP, BUT IT LOOKS LIKE THEY BOTH GOT AWAY.

WELL, DO ME A FAVOR... SEE IF YOU CAN TRACK THEM DOWN, WOULD YOU?

I DON'T KNOW, ELVIS. WE'RE SUPPOSED TO BE WORKING THIS CHUPACABRA CASE. I DON'T THINK WAYNE'S GONNA LIKE IT HE FINDS OUT WE BEEN FREE-LANCING FOR YOU GUYS.
YEAH, I GET THAT, BUT I'M KIND OF IN A BIND OVER HERE.

WE'VE GOT A GIANT MONSTER IN OUR WAY.

ELVIS, GET OUT OF HERE!
I CAN HELP YOU!
HE'S AFTER YOU, NOT ME. IF YOU GO, I THINK THIS THING MIGHT SETTLE DOWN.

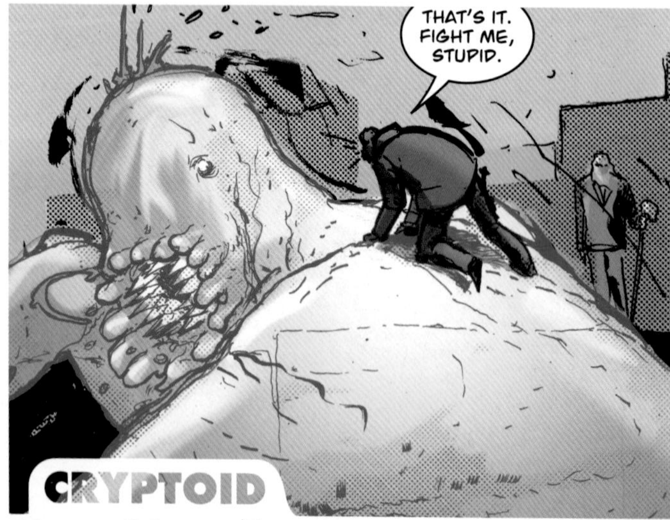

CRYPTOID

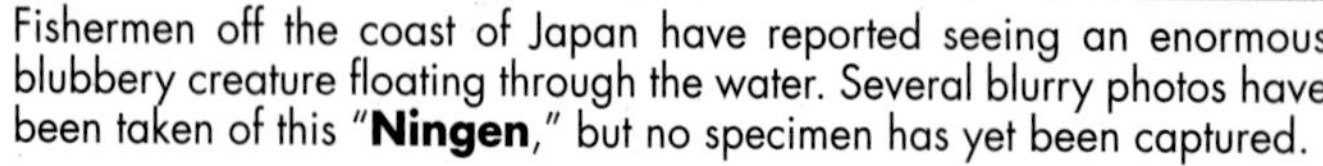

Fishermen off the coast of Japan have reported seeing an enormous blubbery creature floating through the water. Several blurry photos have been taken of this "**Ningen**," but no specimen has yet been captured.

C'MON, BABY, PICK UP. PICK UP.

DAMNIT, WHERE ARE YOU?

HEY, OVER HERE, MAN.
RAIN?
GET LOST, TWERP.

NO, YOU GOTTA HELP ME, MAN.
MY SISTER'S GONNA KILL ME.

NOT MY PROBLEM. SOMEBODY'S TRYING TO KILL MY GIRLFRIEND AND I DON'T KNOW WHERE SHE IS.
THAT'S A LITTLE MORE IMPORTANT TO ME RIGHT NOW THAN WHATEVER SIBLING RIVALRY YOU'VE GOT GOING ON.
OH, YEAH?

I KNOW WHERE SHE IS, MAN.
I CAN TAKE YOU TO HER.

OH, GOOD. THERE YOU ARE.
DIDN'T YOU HEAR ME CALLING?

GINGER? ARE YOU OKAY?

WHOA!
SLISH

GINGER!
YOU COULD'VE CUT ME WITH THAT!

WHAT THE HELL ARE YOU DOING?

YOU'RE NOT...
YOU'RE NOT HOME, ARE YOU?

OH, GOD!

OH, MY GOD!

STOP IT!
JUST... JUST STOP IT!

GINGER, DON'T MAKE ME SHOOT YOU!

GHUFF!

OH, SHIT.

OH.
OH, GOD.

GINGER, PLEASE.

GINGER, YOU KNOW ME.
WE'RE FRIENDS. YOU DON'T WANT TO HURT ME.

I *KNOW* YOU DON'T WANT TO HURT ME.

BLAM

THE LODGE
I CAN'T BELIEVE YOU JUST GAVE HIM YOUR GUN.
WE'RE STILL ALIVE BECAUSE I GAVE HIM MY GUN.

WE SHOULD SEE IF THERE'S ANYTHING HERE WE CAN USE TO ESCAPE.
LOVELY.
THIS MIGHT HELP. HE DIDN'T GET MY BACKUP GUN.

WHAT I DON'T GET... THE FAIRIES HAD DACHSHUND AND HIS MEN PINNED DOWN HERE, RIGHT?
SO HOW DID DACHSHUND GET THE JUMP ON THE FAIRIES? HE HAD TO HAVE LURED THEM CLOSE.

I THINK I KNOW...

HE USED HIS OWN PEOPLE AS BAIT.
"ARE YOU TOO SCARED TO FIGHT ME YOURSELF?"

LITTLE TOKYO

COME DOWN HERE AND DO YOUR OWN DIRTY WORK, GILLY!

YOU DON'T UNDERSTAND ANYTHING, DO YOU, BROTHER?

THIS ISN'T MY WORK. THIS IS THE WORK OF THE ENTIRE WORLD.

IT'S THE HUMANS WHO CAN'T COOPERATE, THEY'RE THE ONES FLAILING BLINDLY ABOUT IN THE DARK.

THE REST OF US -- EVERY OTHER CREATURE ON THIS PLANET -- WE WORK TOGETHER. THE REST OF US UNDERSTAND THAT EVERYTHING IN THIS WORLD IS CONNECTED. WE SEE THE CYCLE OF LIFE.

AND, BY THE WAY, I HAVEN'T CALLED MYSELF GILGAMESH IN MORE THAN A CENTURY.

NAMES ARE SUCH A HUMAN THING, DON'T YOU THINK?

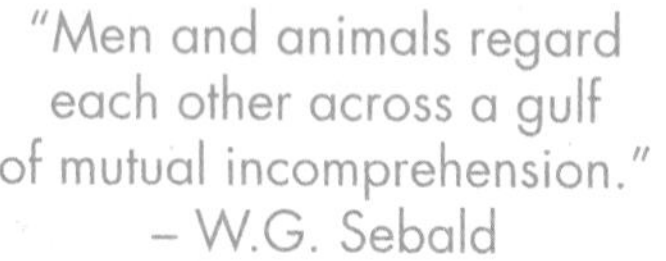
"Men and animals regard each other across a gulf of mutual incomprehension."
– W.G. Sebald

HAHAHAHAHA
THIS BIG FELLOW? HE'S JUST HERE TO DISTRACT YOU.
HE CERTAINLY ISN'T A MONSTER.

I THOUGHT I'D ALREADY MADE IT CLEAR THAT THE ONLY REAL MONSTERS ARE HUMAN BEINGS.
HUMANS KILL EACH OTHER ALL THE TIME, AND FOR NO REASON AT ALL.
THEY **LOVE** TO KILL!

IN FACT, IT WAS CHILD'S PLAY FOR ME TO SUGGEST THAT YOUR CLOSEST FRIEND SHOULD KILL EVERYONE ELSE YOU KNOW.

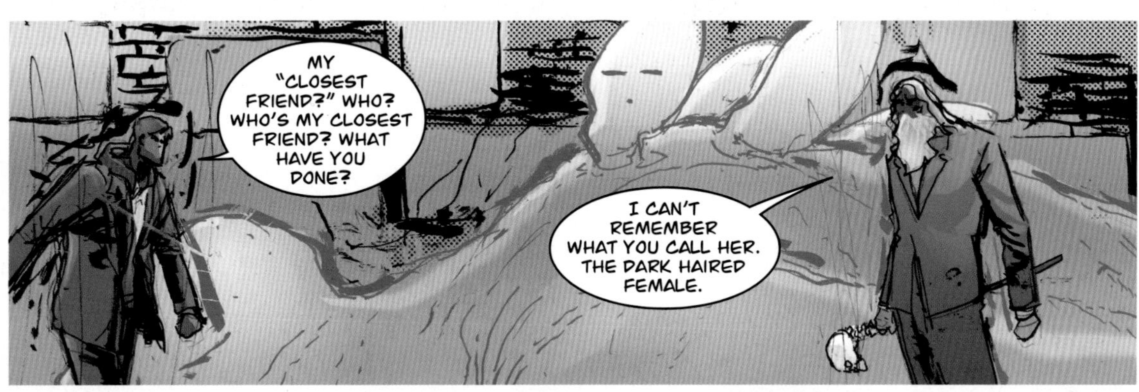
MY "CLOSEST FRIEND?" WHO? WHO'S MY CLOSEST FRIEND? WHAT HAVE YOU DONE?
I CAN'T REMEMBER WHAT YOU CALL HER. THE DARK HAIRED FEMALE.

I PLANTED A SIMPLE POST-HYPNOTIC SUGGESTION...
TOLD HER TO KILL EVERYONE YOU LOVED. AND THEN KILL HERSELF.
I'M SURE SHE'S BEEN ACTIVATED BY NOW.

GINGER? YOU DID THAT TO GINGER?
OH, NO.

YEAH. BELINDA? YEAH, I'VE GOT ONE OF THEM WITH ME NOW. SO IT'S JUST THE GIRL THAT'S IN THE WIND.
HEY, SHE'S SHOPPING WITH HER FRIEND, YO.
WHO? YOUR SISTER'S SHOPPING?
NO, YOUR GIRLFRIEND. SHE'S SHOPPING WITH THAT FREAKY CHICK WHO'S BONING THE BIGFOOT.
OUCH!
THOSE ARE MY FRIENDS, ASSHOLE.
YOU NEED BACKUP OVER THERE?
I DON'T, NO. BUT YOU MIGHT WANNA HELP PROOF. NADINE MIGHT BE ABLE TO DO SOMETHING AGAINST THAT WATER MONSTER THING OUT THERE.
I DIDN'T MEAN NOTHIN'. I'M HELPING, SEE? MY BOYS HAVE BEEN FOLLOWING ALL YOU LOT. I KNOW WHERE EVERY-BODY IS ALL THE TIME.
RIGHT. SO YOU COULD KILL US.
NO WAY, MAN. I WAS ONLY EVER GONNA KILL THE BIGFOOT. THAT SKIN'S VALUABLE, MAN. BIG MONEY.
ELVIS?

ELVIS? WE'RE HEADED YOUR DIRECTION.
SOMETHING IS BAD.

SOMETHING IS BAD WITH MINE SKIN-BOY!
GIVE ME THAT! LET ME TALK! DO YOU SMELL IT? DO YOU SMELL? SOMETHING IS BAD!
HEY, BACK OFF!

RIGHT HERE, MAN. YOUR LADIES ARE RIGHT IN THERE.
HELP!
BELLA!?!

SHE ALL RIGHT. CRAZY PERSON INSIDE TRYING TO KILL US ALL.
RAIN, CALL AN AMBULANCE. GET HELP.
WHAT'S YOUR PROBLEM? STOP IT!

THE OTHER LADY? WHERE'S THE OTHER LADY? HER FRIEND?
SHE A CRAZY LADY. SHE HAS THE GUN.

ELVIS? WHAT'S GOING ON THERE? NADINE'S GOING NUTS OVER HERE!

GINGER?

GINGER, HONEY? ARE YOU OKAY?
HEY, BABE, WHERE'S THE BAD GUY?

BLAM
BLAM
BLAM

GINGER?

NO!!!

SOMEWHERE IN TIBET

TWO MONTHS AGO

KNOCK
KNOCK

GOOD MORNING, MARC.
ARE WE GOING? IS IT TIME?

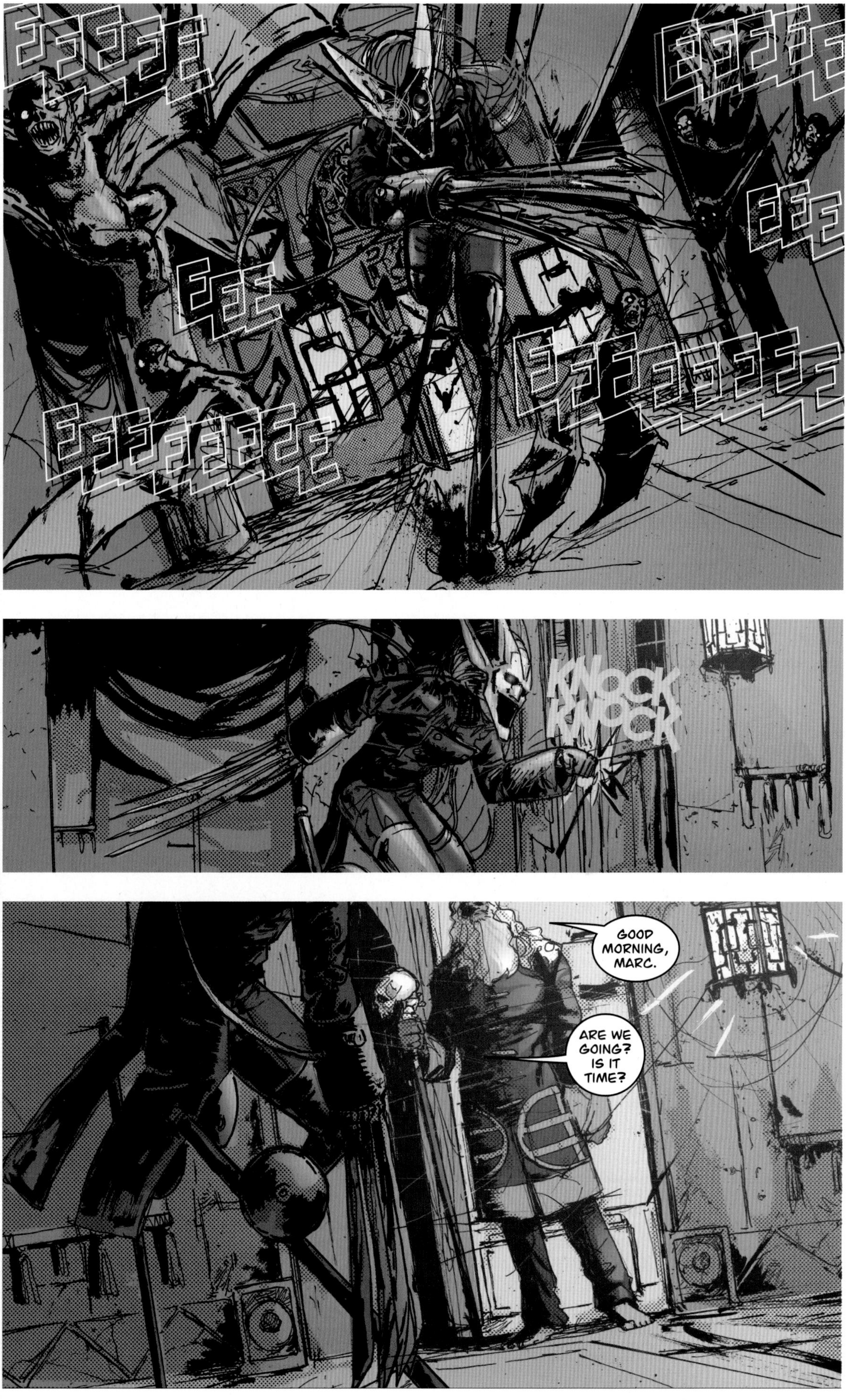

SO EAGER. SUCH ENTHUSIASM. YES, MARC, IT IS TIME.
THE CHAIN OF EVENTS HAS BEEN SET IN MOTION. THE FINGER IS ON ITS WAY TO MY BROTHER EVEN NOW.
GOOD. THIS SKIN IS TIGHT. I WANT SOMETHING NEW.

WE'RE IN THE ENDGAME AT LAST, MY STUDENTS.
AND WE ALL HAVE ROLES TO PLAY.
EVERY ONE OF US.

LITTLE TOKYO: NOW

GINGER?
I DON'T KNOW...
I DON'T KNOW WHAT'S HAPPENING...
BUT I LOVE YOU AND I KNOW THIS CAN'T BE YOU DOING THIS.

IF YOU'RE... UM, IF YOU CAN HEAR ME...
BELLA'S OKAY, BABE. DON'T WORRY. YOU DIDN'T HURT HER.
EVERY-THING'S GONNA BE OKAY.
BUT IN CASE THIS DOESN'T... I MEAN, I DON'T KNOW HOW BAD--

JUST DO ME A FAVOR AND TELL HIM ABOUT ME, OKAY?
MAKE SURE HE KNOWS I... WELL, I--
DAMN, THIS ISN'T...

SOMEBODY NEEDS TO TELL ME WHAT'S HAPPENING HERE.
THE WAY SHE'S ACTING... I THINK MAYBE IT'S SOME SORT OF EXTREME POST-HYPNOTIC SUGGESTION.

SHE WAS BEING CONTROLLED?
I THINK SO. BUT WHO COULD DO THAT?
WHO **WOULD** DO THAT?

I HAVE A PRETTY GOOD IDEA.
IS THERE ANYTHING YOU CAN DO TO SNAP HER OUT OF IT?

I CAN TRY.
YEAH, DO THAT.
INTERCEPTED A CALL ON THIS PLACE. THERE'S A BLOODY JAPANESE GUY OUT THERE YELLING ABOUT HIS SHOP GETTING SHOT UP. COPS ARE GONNA BE HERE ANY MINUTE.

WHERE--?
I TRIED CALLIN' WAYNE TO SEE IF MAYBE WE COULD DIVERT THE COPS, BUT I COULDN'T GET--
OH, SHIT.

NO! DON'T LOOK!
KEEP BACK!
MY SKINBOY!

MY SKINBOY!

MY SKINBOY!
AW, CRAP.

GET GINGER OUT OF HERE!
"WHAT IN HOLY HELL IS GOING ON HERE?"

Crossdressing does not necessarily indicate homosexuality. Women who dress as men and mimic male attributes are commonly called "drag kings," although the term "drag queen" is used far more often for their crossdressing counterparts.

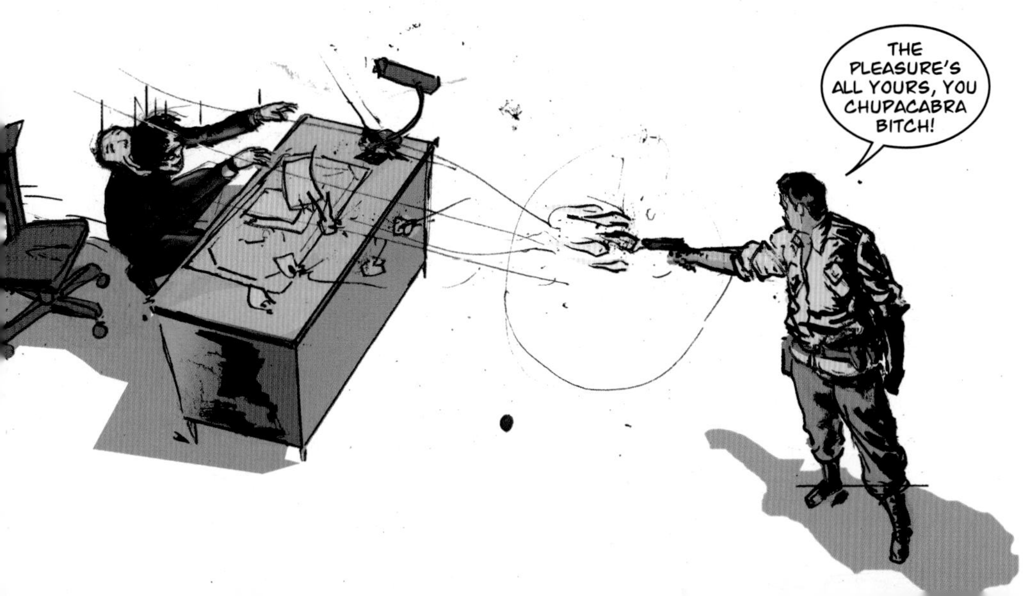

CAREFUL NOW. YOU'LL DAMAGE THE SKINS.

THOSE ARE SOLDIERS' SKINS. *HUMAN SOLDIERS!*

YOU KILLED THOSE MEN!

YES, BUT I'M WILLING TO TRADE. I LIKE YOUR SKIN BETTER.

NO GUNS, SILLY BOY.

A BLADE?

TEE HEE!
YOU CAN'T HURT ME WITH THAT LITTLE THING.

MAYBE NOT. BUT I CAN MAKE DAMN SURE YOU DON'T USE MY SKIN, BITCH!

NOOO!
HEH.

SUCH A WASTE.
BUT SUCH IS LIFE, I SUPPOSE...

LET'S AT LEAST SEE HOW YOU TASTE.

CLICK
MY GUESS IS HE'S TOUGH AND STRINGY.
LET'S GET OFF HIM NOW. SLOWLY.

I WONDERED WHERE YOU'D GOT TO, HAVEN-MAN. AND THE WAYNE-THING TOO. HIDING FROM ME?
MY THANKS, GENTLEMEN. WHAT TOOK YOU?

WE WERE DETAINED OR WE'D HAVE BEEN HERE SOONER.

I SHOULD HAVE BEEN HERE.

I SHOULD HAVE COME WITH YOU.
OR KEPT YOU THERE WITH ME.
WE BOTH WOULD HAVE BEEN BETTER OFF IF YOU'D STAYED WITH ME.

YOU'RE ONE OF THE BEST PEOPLE I'VE EVER MET. BRAVE AND KIND AND SELFLESS.
I'M SO SORRY I LET THIS HAPPEN TO YOU.
I WON'T FORGET YOU, SHERIFF.

OH, MY GOD! WHAT HAPPENED?
GINGER--
HE ISN'T--

SHE DOESN'T KNOW.
OH, NO. OH, NO. OH, NO.
LET ME UP.
WHAT, UM--?
DAMNIT, I DON'T--

HERE, TRADE ME PLACES.
JUST COME HERE. NADINE WILL BE A GOOD GIRL. AND IF SHE GETS OUT OF LINE AGAIN...

I WILL BE GOOD.
COME HERE, SWEET-HEART.

SHE HAS NO IDEA. SHE REMEMBERS FIGHTING HER EX-BOYFRIEND AND THEN...
WHO KILLED MY SKIN-BOY, GULLIVER?
DON'T WORRY. WE'RE GONNA GET THE GUY WHO'S REALLY RESPONSIBLE FOR THIS.

SO, IS SHE STILL--?
IT'S GOING TO TAKE SOME TIME. I'LL WORK WITH HER.
SHE THOUGHT WE WERE MONSTERS. SHE JUST... IN HER MIND SHE SAW SOMETHING COMPLETELY DIFFERENT.

SHE THOUGHT SHE WAS PROTECTING US.

I DIDN'T THINK IT WAS POSSIBLE TO MAKE SOMEONE DO SOMETHING THEY WOULDN'T--
I DON'T REALLY KNOW WHAT'S POSSIBLE. AS FAR AS I KNOW, NOBODY DOES. HYPNOSIS ISN'T AN EXACT SCIENCE.
AND IF PO HAS THE SAME SCENT-BASED ABILITIES YOU DO...

IF SHE'S--
COME OUT HERE, BROTHER!
COME OUT AND TALK TO ME!

IT'S BAD OUT THERE, MAN!
I NEVER SEEN SUCH THINGS.
SONOFA--

HOW MANY TIMES DO I HAVE TO FIGHT THIS GUY?
IF YOU WON'T COME OUT, I'LL HAVE TO COME IN AFTER YOU, BROTHER!

IT'S ALWAYS "I" WITH YOU, JOHN. HAVEN'T YOU LEARNED BY NOW...?

LIFE'S A TEAM EFFORT.

I'M AFRAID YOU WON'T LIKE IT IF I HAVE TO COME IN THERE.

RIGHT...

LET'S END THIS THING.

"If life was fair, Elvis would be alive and all the impersonators would be dead."
– Johnny Carson

YOU DID
THIS.

GINGER? WHAT ARE YOU--? **WHOA!**

"WHAT SHOULD WE DO WITH HER?"

SHE'S NOT HUMAN. WE CAN'T JUST TURN HER OVER TO THE POLICE.
I SAY WE HAVE HER FOR LUNCH.
THE LODGE

YOU DISGUST ME, DACHSHUND.
HEH!

LUNCH SOUNDS DELIGHTFUL, GENTLEMEN.

BUT I'M AFRAID I WON'T BE ABLE TO MAKE IT TODAY.

SHOOT HER. SHOOT!

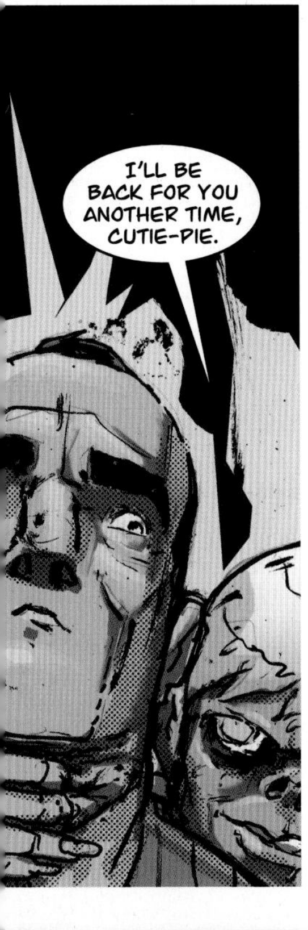
I'LL BE BACK FOR YOU ANOTHER TIME, CUTIE-PIE.

SLURP

STOP HER!

CRASH

WHY DIDN'T YOU SHOOT?

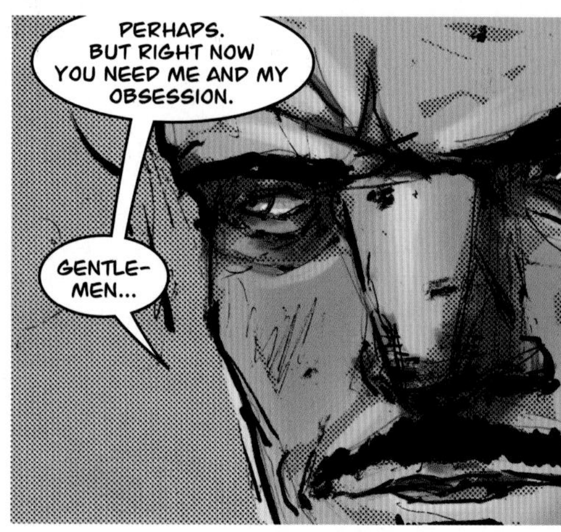

I SUGGEST YOU ARM YOUR-SELVES. THERE'S A DANGEROUS CREATURE OUT THERE THAT HAS TO BE BROUGHT DOWN.

WE'VE GOT OUR-SELVES A HUNT!

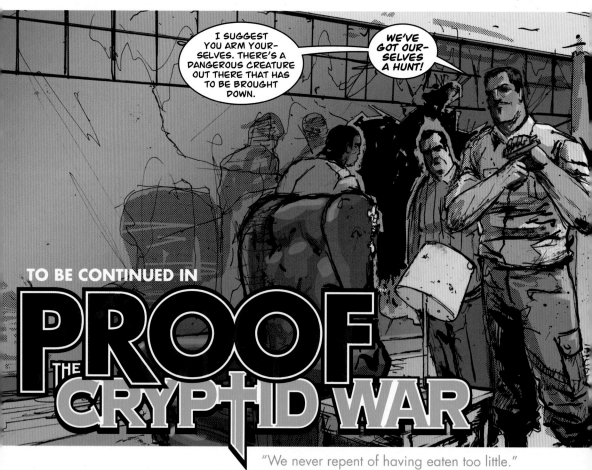

TO BE CONTINUED IN

PROOF™ THE CRYPTID WAR

"We never repent of having eaten too little."
– Thomas Jefferson

TOO MANY OF 'EM!

DAMNIT!
WATCH OUT, LADY!
SLISH

AH!

WHEW

I HAD IT. I WAS FINE.
OF COURSE. I WAS BORED, THAT'S ALL.

NEEDED SOMETHING TO DO.
GOOD. LONG AS THAT'S SETTLED THEN.

HEY, WE GET OUT OF THIS ALIVE, WHAT YOU DOING TONIGHT?

COME FIND ME AND WE'LL SEE.

GINGER, STOP!
YOU CRUSHED JOHN BACK THERE. YOU NEED TO LET THE OTHERS HANDLE THIS.

I KNOW YOU'RE ANGRY. I KNOW YOU'VE BEEN THROUGH A LOT--

YOU DON'T KNOW SHIT!!
YOU DON'T HAVE A FUCKING CLUE WHAT I'M GOING THROUGH!

I'M SO SORRY. OF COURSE I DON'T KNOW.
OF COURSE I DON'T.

I KILLED HIM, BELLA. I KILLED ELVIS.

HEY.
IS SHE--?
NO, SHE'S NOT OKAY.

IS THERE ANYTHING--? I MEAN, WHAT CAN I DO?

JOHN...
YOU HAVE TO KILL MI-CHEN-PO.

WHAT?

HE KILLED ELVIS. HE VIOLATED GINGER.
YES, BUT--
JOHN, HE'S NOT GOING TO STOP UNTIL WE'RE ALL DEAD. EVERYBODY CLOSE TO YOU. HE'S GOING TO KILL ALL OF US AND YOU WON'T BE ABLE TO STOP HIM UNLESS YOU DO IT NOW.

NO, I CAN STOP HIM. THERE ARE OTHER WAYS TO--

JOHN, SHE'S PREGNANT!

GINGER'S PREGNANT AND HER BABY'S FATHER IS DEAD.
WE'RE THE ONLY FAMILY THAT BABY'S GOING TO HAVE. YOU HAVE TO STEP UP NOW.

YOU HAVE TO PROTECT YOUR FAMILY.

GULLIVER?

POPLAR FOREST : 1814
GULLIVER?
SIR... MISTER PRESIDENT...
IS SHE--?
CORDELIA WILL BE FINE.

BUT YOU COULD HAVE HURT HER VERY BADLY. I DON'T THINK YOU REALIZE HOW MUCH BIGGER AND STRONGER YOU ARE.

I KNOW, SIR. I DIDN'T MEAN TO...
DON'T WORRY. I'M GOING AWAY. I'LL GO BACK TO OREGON AND FIND MY REAL FAMILY AND I WON'T--
WELL, YOU MAY CERTAINLY DO THAT IF YOU WISH...
BUT I THINK IT MIGHT BE A GOOD IDEA IF YOU APOLOGIZED TO CORDELIA FIRST.

SHE DOESN'T... SIR, I WORRY THAT I MIGHT HURT HER AGAIN.
NOW WHY WOULD YOU DO THAT?

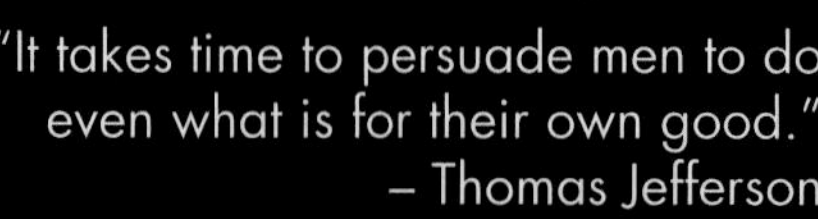

"It takes time to persuade men to do even what is for their own good."
– Thomas Jefferson

TO BE CONTINUED IN

PROOF™

Poplar Forest

DAD NEVER LOVED YOU.
FUNNY, THAT'S WHAT HE SAID ABOUT YOU.

YOU'RE LYING.
AM I? WHAT'D YOU EVER DO FOR HIM?
I GAVE HIM THE LOCH NESS CREATURE. ALL YOU EVER GAVE HIM WAS FAIRIES AND GNOMES.

AND BROWNIES. I GAVE HIM BROWNIES.
WELL, I HEARD YOU TRIED TO SURPRISE HIM WITH THE DINOSAURS AND THAT WEIRD LITTLE THING THAT TELLS THE FUTURE.
I DID TRY. THAT DIDN'T WORK OUT.

AT LEAST YOU TRIED. HE COULD'VE GIVEN YOU SOME CREDIT FOR THAT.
THANKS. YOU KNOW, THERE'S A WHOLE LOT OF CRITTERS OUT HERE WE COULD BAG FOR HIS BIRTHDAY. MAYBE WE COULD--

...

AUTUMN LADY, I KNOW IT WASN'T YOU KILLED MINE SKIN BOY. YOU WERE AT THE PLACE WITH ME.
I WILL LET YOU LIVE.

BLAM

OH, DAMNIT.
DAD'S GONNA BLAME ME FOR THIS, I KNOW IT.

THE THING ABOUT CHUPACABRAS...

YOU SHOULD ALWAYS LOOK UNDER OUR SKIN BEFORE YOU TURN YOUR BACK ON US!

HOW DID YOU THINK THIS WOULD END?

I MEAN, WHAT WERE YOU THINKING?
YOU'RE GONNA KILL MY FRIENDS, MY FAMILY, AND THEN I'M GOING TO, WHAT? GO AWAY WITH YOU TO... TO WHEREVER?
THIS IS SOME BIG REUNION? SOME HAPPY ENDING FOR YOU?

WHEN I WAS ALONE...
WHEN I HAD NO ONE ELSE...
I HAD YOU. YOU WERE MY BROTHER, MY FAMILY, MY WORLD.
I THOUGHT MAYBE... MAYBE IF THERE WAS NOBODY ELSE FOR YOU NOW...

BUT, GILLY, IT DOESN'T WORK THAT WAY.

IF YOU KILLED EVERYONE I LOVE... IF YOU SUCCEEDED IN THAT... I WOULD NEVER REST UNTIL YOU WERE DEAD.
YOU'RE GOING TO KILL ME NOW, AREN'T YOU?

I DON'T WANT TO.
BUT I THINK I HAVE TO.

TO BE CONTINUED IN

PROOF THE SQUID AND THE MOUNTAIN

"An injured friend is the bitterest of foes."
– Thomas Jefferson

EPILOGUE

INISHBOFIN, COUNTY DONEGAL, IRELAND

FIVE YEARS LATER

"I like the dreams of the future better than the history of the past." – Thomas Jefferson

BY MICHAEL HOSKI
ART: RILEY ROSSMO

LEGAL NAME: John Prufrock
OTHER NAMES: "Proof," Gulliver
OCCUPATION: Federal agent; former circus performer
NATIONALITY: USA
LEGAL STATUS: No criminal record
BIRTHPLACE: Unrevealed
RELATIVES: Robert Winstone (adopted father, deceased), Mi-Chen-Po (Gilgamesh, adopted brother)
MARITAL STATUS: Unmarried
MEMBERSHIP: The Lodge; formerly Swift Brothers Circus
RESIDENCE: The Lodge, Washington, USA
EXTENT OF EDUCATION: Unrevealed
FIRST APPEARANCE: *Negative Burn #7* (December, 2006)

BACKGROUND: On December 25th, 1805, Meriwether Lewis and William Clark, in the midst of their expedition of th Northwestern United States, encountered a member of the cryptozoological species ("Cryptid") commonly called Sasquatch (or "Bigfoot") at Fort Clatsop, Oregon. Amazingly, the Sasquatch had adopted the English language from over-hearing soldiers in the fort. Impressed by his size, Lewis and Clark named him "Gulliver," after the protagonist of Jonathan Swift's *Gulliver's Travels*. Gulliver's life and family origins prio to meeting Lewis and Clark was a mystery, seemingly even to Gulliver himself. Lewis and Clark introduced Gulliver to US President Thomas Jefferson, who made Gulliver one of his closest companions. From Jefferson, Gulliver learned lessons i etiquette, particularly the importance of grooming and fashio thereafter adopting human clothing and customs. After Jefferson's death in 1826, Gulliver was alone for a time until he met Robert Winstone, owner of the Swift Brothers Circus. Winstone had obtained a close relation to the Sasquatch family (commonly called Yeti) and was inspired to name him Gilgamesh to echo Gulliver's name. Gulliver and Gilgamesh became performers in the circus and were encouraged to thin of each other as brothers with Winstone as their father.

By 1859, the Swift Brothers were touring London, England wi the sideshow attraction Julia Pastrana, a human woman whos hairy complexion was similar to a Sasquatch. Gulliver carried an unrequited love for Julia, but she was married to Thomas Lent. Gulliver and Gilgamesh became embroiled in the search for the serial killer Spring-Heeled Jack alongside Inspector August McKraken. Tragically, Winstone died of heart failure during the case. Gilgamesh could not reconcile his resentment towards humans without Winstone's influence and grew apart from Gulliver, eventually taking to the Tibetan Himalayas unde the name Mi-Chen-Po. Gulliver was grief-stricken when Julia Pastrana died soon after bearing Thomas Lent's son (whom Lent murdered). Although Gulliver inherited the Swift Brothers Circus from Winstone, he sold it to Inspector McKraken and virtually disappeared from human history for decades.

After being sighted in 1969 in the Pacific Northwest of North America, Gulliver – now using the name John Prufrock – was recruited by the joint Canadian-US operation The Lodge. Based on a vast wilderness preserve in Washington, The Lodg was tasked with finding and preserving Cryptids. Prufrock, or "Proof," was one of The Lodge's founding agents and their ambassador. Proof agreed to assist the Lodge partially in hopes of locating other members of his species. He developed a strong friendship with Wayne Russet, with whom he found the legendary Cryptid the Dover Demon. Proof also took a Pallas Cat from the Lodge as his pet, naming it Felix.

Proof frequently worked alongside human agents, including C.K. Dexter Haven. In recent years he took on his third partner, FBI agent Ginger Brown. With Brown, Proof investigated a Chupacabra, the so-called "Mexican Bigfoot," but found the creature had no actual ties to his species. Proof also rescued a baby dinosaur in the Congo from the Cryptid-eating Colonel Dachsund, who attempted to add Proof to his menu. After working alongside the Savage Dragon in a case involving the Thunderbirds, Proof learned Julia Pastrana's preserved remains had been discovered; having found closure by giving Julia a proper burial, Proof entered into a relationship with Isabella Bay, a counselor at the Lodge. Unfortunately, the Lodge was soon torn apart by internal strife as team head Leander Wight mysteriously disappeared. When Proof received a finger which proved to share his genetic heritage, he took a leave from The Lodge to investigate, hoping to finally discover the whereabouts of his birth family.

CAPABILITIES: Proof can control the pheromones emitted from his body, usually employing them to relax people in his vicinity or to drive them away; using this ability he is able to travel in public without drawing undue attention and can diffuse tense situations in the course of his work. Proof has extraordinary olfactory senses, enabling him to track people by their scent. Proof is immune to most poisons, but is still susceptible to viral infections. He is an agile climber and has surprisingly quick reflexes for a person of his size. Proof is an enormously quick study at grasping other languages, having demonstrated a grasp of English and Norwegian.

HEIGHT: 7'6"
WEIGHT: 850 lbs.
EYE COLOR: Light brown
HAIR/FUR COLOR: Brown

PARAPHERNALIA: Proof wears specially crafted size 29 shoes made of Stingray leather. He usually carries a cell phone.

GINGER BROWN

LEGAL NAME: Ginger Brown
OTHER NAMES: None
OCCUPATION: Federal agent
NATIONALITY: Puerto Rico/USA
LEGAL STATUS: No criminal record
BIRTHPLACE: Puerto Rico
RELATIVES: Unrevealed
MARITAL STATUS: Unmarried
MEMBERSHIP: The Lodge, FBI
RESIDENCE: The Lodge, Washington, USA
EXTENT OF EDUCATION: FBI Academy graduate
FIRST APPEARANCE: Proof #1 (October, 2007)

HEIGHT: 5′10″
WEIGHT: 130 lbs.
EYE COLOR: Brown
HAIR COLOR: Brown

BACKGROUND: Dedicated to law enforcement and crime solving, Ginger Brown joined the FBI, eager to use her gifts in deduction. Ginger was assigned to work with NYPD Lt. Belinda Drake in Manhattan and became romantically involved with fellow agent Marc Ravello. During a supposedly routine assignment where criminals were robbing a diamond store outlet, Ginger encountered Joseph Loew, a centuries-old Golem who had recently been reawakened and defended the premises from the robbers. Unable to prove Joseph's existence but unwilling to let go of the case, Ginger's persistence drew the attention of the Lodge, a joint US-Canadian operation which serves as ambassadors to "Cryptids" (creatures believed extinct or cryptozoological). Lodge director Leander Wight assigned Ginger as partner John "Proof" Prufrock, a Bigfoot who had been with the Lodge since its founding and hoped to find information on his own species.

Ginger was quickly thrust into action, accompanying Proof to Leeward, Minnesota to investigate a sighting of a Chupacabra, which Proof thought might be related to the Bigfoot. During the investigation, Ginger befriended local sheriff Elvis Chestnut, whose mother became one of the Chupacabra's victims. Ginger helped Elvis cope with the strange and ghastly world he had wandered into, bringing him into the Lodge. Ginger soon found she was well-suited to the Lodge, having an insatiable curiosity about how the world works and realizing through the Lodge she was unearthing secrets which had been long hidden.

Returning to Manhattan with Elvis to complete the investigation into Joseph, Ginger was reunited with Marc, who proposed marriage to her. Ginger blew off his proposal, instead venturing into Manhattan's sewers to find Joseph Loew. During the pursuit of Joseph, Ginger encountered Mi-Chen-Po, Proof's adopted brother, who implanted a posthypnotic suggestion in Ginger, then removed her memory of their encounter. While following Ginger into the sewers, Marc lost his right hand to an alligator and became bitter over losing Ginger and his hand, turning him into an enemy of the Lodge. Ginger and Elvis began dating just as the Lodge was overrun by US government forces who assumed authority over the operation, exposing Leander Wight as an imposter. Having finally received evidence of a familial Bigfoot, Proof left the Lodge to investigate. Ginger left the Lodge with Proof and Elvis, and is helping to investigate Proof's origins.

CAPABILITIES: Ginger has extensive training in law enforcement and keeps in excellent physical shape. Although Ginger is an experienced marksman, she tends to pull to the right when shooting. Ginger speaks English and Spanish.

PARAPHERNALIA: Ginger usually carries a Glock 22 pistol and occasionally a Smith & Wesson Model 13 revolver.

ELVIS CHESTNUT

BACKGROUND: Elvis Chestnut was the elected St. Louis County sheriff of Leeward, Minnesota and was especially devoted to his mother, Nadine. Unfortunately, Elvis' path crossed that of a Chupacabra, a creature which wears the skins of its victims. After picking up the Chupacabra in the skin of Jeanette Levy, a missing hiker, Elvis inadvertently set up paramedic Nancy Wallace as its next victim when Nancy went to check on "Jeanette" in a restroom. Wearing Nancy's skin, the Chupacabra accessed Elvis' home and found Nadine near death, suffering from cardiac arrest; the Chupacabra donned Nadine's skin. Elvis was quickly brought up to speed by Ginger Brown, FBI and agent of the Lodge, a joint US-Canadian operation to liaise with "Cryptids" (creatures either extinct or thought cryptozoological). Ginger's Bigfoot partner John "Proof" Prufrock collared the Chupacabra and deposited it in the Habitat on the Lodge's grounds. Elvis was distraught both by his mother's death and at the Chupacabra wearing her skin, performing a grotesque masquerade of her behavior.

With his life in ruins, Elvis resigned as county sheriff and went to live on the Lodge's grounds. He was quickly accepted by the other Lodge employees, who insisted on calling him "sheriff." Although Elvis made an attempt to kill the Chupacabra soon after his arrival, it outfought him and he needed Lodge director Leander Wight to save him. Elvis soon learned to cope with the creature's existence. Elvis joined the Lodge agents in the field, helping to rescue a baby dinosaur from the Cryptid-eating Colonel Dachshund. Soon after, Proof took Elvis shopping in Seattle, urging him to adopt stylish clothing and to trim his normally elaborately coiffed hair.

Elvis joined Ginger on an assignment in Manhattan to find the golem Joseph Loew, during which he met Ginger's boyfriend Marc Ravello. Following the mission, the Dover Demon, a prophetic creature, informed Elvis that Marc would kill him. Soon after, Elvis began dating Ginger; when the Lodge's operations were taken over directly by the US government, Elvis moved to Japantown with Ginger to help find Proof's birth family.

HEIGHT: 6′ **WEIGHT:** 145 lbs.
EYE COLOR: Light blue **HAIR COLOR:** Black

BY MICHAEL HOSKIN ART: RILEY ROSSMO

LEGAL NAME: Elvis Aaron Chestnut
OTHER NAMES: "Sheriff"
OCCUPATION: Federal agent; former St. Louis County sheriff
NATIONALITY: USA
LEGAL STATUS: No criminal record
BIRTHPLACE: Leeward, Minnesota
RELATIVES: Nadine Chestnut (mother, deceased)
MARITAL STATUS: Unmarried
MEMBERSHIP: The Lodge
RESIDENCE: The Lodge, Washington, USA
EXTENT OF EDUCATION: High school graduate
FIRST APPEARANCE: Proof #2 (November, 2007)

CAPABILITIES: Elvis is an experienced law enforcement officer with some skill at firearms.

PARAPHERNALIA: Elvis occasionally carries a firearm from the Lodge armory.

THE DOVER DEMON

BACKGROUND: The so-called "Dover Demon" was the name of a cryptozoological specimen ("Cryptid") which is actually the larval form of another Cryptid, the Mothman. Larval versions of this Cryptid's species have been active through human history, notably the one dubbed "Madam Wormwood" who was employed as fortune teller with the Swift Brothers Circus in England circa 1859. The best-known Mothman sightings occurred in West Virginia, 1966, and were believed by many cryptozoologists to have been an attempt by the creature to warn humans of an impending bridge collapse.

On April 22, 1977, several teenagers in Dover, Massachusetts caught sight of a larval creature who was soon dubbed "the Dover Demon." Word of its existence swiftly attracted agents of the Lodge, a joint US-Canadian organization which helps protect Cryptids and serves as ambassadors to their species. Agents John "Proof" Prufrock and Wayne Russet located the Dover Demon in the woods surrounding Dover and brought the Cryptid back to the Lodge's wilderness preserve. In the decades which followed, the Dover Demon became a familiar sight to the denizens and agents of the Lodge, regaling any and all beings within earshot (including Dodo birds) with its prophetic warnings of the future.

When the Lodge formed a mission to the Democratic Republic of the Congo to rescue a young dinosaur from Cryptid-eating Colonel Dachshund, the Dover Demon stole aboard their airplane. The Dover Demon was captured and nearly consumed by Dachshund, but agents Ginger Brown and Elvis Chestnut rescued it. The Dover Demon showed a particular interest in Elvis subsequently, delivering a warning to him that Ginger's ex-boyfriend Marc Ravello would kill him. Eventually, the Dover Demon completed its larval stage and shed its skin, transforming into a Mothman. The discovery of the Demon's skin led Elvis and Ginger to assume a Chupacabra had devoured it, but it soon reintroduced itself to the Lodge's staff; the Dover Demon remains a guest of the Lodge.

LEGAL STATUS: Ward of The Lodge
BIRTHPLACE: Dover, Massachusetts
RELATIVES: None known
MARITAL STATUS: Unrevealed
MEMBERSHIP: None
RESIDENCE: The Lodge, Washington DC
EXTENT OF EDUCATION: Unrevealed
FIRST APPEARANCE: *Proof* #2 (November, 2007)

CAPABILITIES: As a Mothman, the Dove[r] Demon possesses large chitinous wings which allow it to fly. In its larval stage, the Dover Demon could see into the future an[d] would relate portions of its findings to others. Although events in the Dover Demon's prophecies would apparently always occur as stated, they would not necessarily transpire in the most obvious fashion. It is unrevealed whether the Dove[r] Demon can still summon visions as a Mothman. In both its forms, the Dover Demon has no visible mouth; its precise means of forming speech and consuming food is unrevealed.

PARAPHERNALIA: None.

LEGAL NAME: None
OTHER NAMES: Mothman
OCCUPATION: Associate of the Lodge
NATIONALITY: Inapplicable
HEIGHT (as Mothman): 7'7"
WEIGHT (as Mothman): 130 lbs.
HAIR COLOR (as Mothman): Black
EYE COLOR: Green

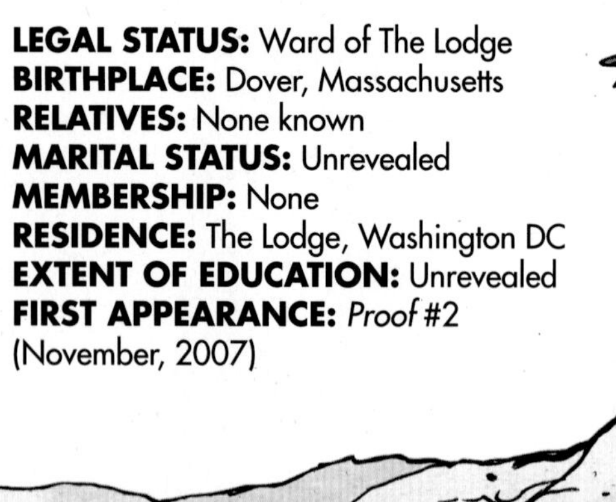

ACKGROUND: Qi is the only known example of ı "ink monkey," believed to be the smallest family of 'imates in history. Because so little is known (or can ; proven) about the ink monkeys, they are consid- ed cryptozoological by most scientists. Allegedly, e domesticated ink monkeys were employed by ribes and other great thinkers to prepare their inks ıd brushes. Ink monkeys would sleep inside the 'awers of their masters' desks when not required. ıe great calligrapher and philosopher Zhu Xi 130-1200 AD) kept an ink monkey, but there was) record of its fate following his death.

recent years the ink monkeys were studied by jents of the Lodge, a joint US-Canadian organiza- ɔn which provides a wilderness preserve for Cryp- ls (cryptozoological creatures). While examining the b-basements of the Institute of Forensic Science in slo, Norway, Lodge agent Noel Russet discovered ı ink monkey living inside of a small box; an tached note indicated its name was Qi (meaning the force or energy of nature). The exact connection of Qi to Zhu Xi's ink monkey is unrevealed, as is the aver- age lifespan of an ink monkey; they may prove to be the same entity.

Noel delivered Qi to the Lodge where it quickly took up residence in the office of Lodge director Leander Wight (actually a Chupacabra wearing his skin). When a carnivorous fairy was accidentally set loose in the Lodge's building, Qi captured it with a make- shift lasso and somehow tamed it; thereafter, the fairy behaved peacefully in Qi's presence. Qi also helped the Lodge treat a wounded Andean wolf, demonstrat- ing a surprising knowledge of herbal remedy. Overall, Qi has demonstrated a fastidious nature, concerned with keeping the Lodge's offices organized and harmonious, serving as an unofficial assistant in the director's office. It has continued to reside in the director's office even as the disguised Chupacabra has begun impersonating Wayne Russet.

GAL NAME: Qi
THER NAMES: None
CCUPATION: Inhabitant of the Lodge; former ush assistant
ATIONALITY: Inapplicable
GAL STATUS: Ward of the Lodge
RTHPLACE: Unrevealed, presumed China
LATIVES: None known
ARITAL STATUS: Unrevealed
EMBERSHIP: None
SIDENCE: The Lodge, Washington, DC
TENT OF EDUCATION: Unrevealed
RST APPEARANCE: *Proof* #11 (August, 2008)

HEIGHT: 5"
WEIGHT: 4 oz.
EYE COLOR: Brown
HAIR/FUR COLOR: Brown

CAPABILITIES: Qi is exceptionally talented at wielding human-sized instruments and demonstrates an awareness of his environment which borders on sentience. Although Qi's primary training was in mixing ink, washing brushes and turning pages, he has also proved capable in herbal remedies and lassoing objects.

PARAPHERNALIA: None.

COLONEL DACHSHUND

LEGAL NAME: Werner Dachshund
OTHER NAMES: None
OCCUPATION: Mercenary, hunter
NATIONALITY: USA
LEGAL STATUS: International criminal record
BIRTHPLACE: Unrevealed
RELATIVES: Unidentified daughter
MARITAL STATUS: Unrevealed
MEMBERSHIP: Formerly US Marines
RESIDENCE: The Lodge, Washington, USA
EXTENT OF EDUCATION: US Marine Academy graduate
FIRST APPEARANCE: *Proof* #6 (March, 2008)

HEIGHT: 5'11" **EYE COLOR:** Light blue
WEIGHT: 220 lbs. **HAIR COLOR:** Black (graying)

CAPABILITIES: Colonel Dachshund is a natural leader, a considerable hand-to-hand combatant and marksman with experience from his US Marine training. Dachshund's appetite for Cryptids is insatiable and virtually unrestricted.

PARAPHERNALIA: Colonel Dachshund has used a variety of hunting rifles, machine guns, machetes and pistols.

BY MICHAEL HOSKIN ART: RILEY ROSSMO

BACKGROUND: Formerly an officer in the US Marines, some 30 years ago Colonel Dachshund became enamored with the sensation of eating Crypto-zoological creatures ("Cryptids"). To this end, Dachshund formed a band of roaming mercenaries who hunted Cryptids for sport and meal. Dachshund quickly made enemies with The Lodge, a facility in Washington which served as ambassadors to Cryptid community a[nd] which kept a preserve for numerous species on their grounds. The Lodge placed their agent Henry Kalamb[ayi] within Dachshund's ranks to spy on him, but Dachshun[d] allied with The Lodge's agent Autumn Song to maneuv[er] The Lodge into sending their agent John Prufrock (a Bigfoot) after him, hoping to devour Prufrock.

Dachshund brought his party to the Democratic Republ[ic] of the Congo to hunt the dinosaurs living in its jungles. Successfully slaying two parents for a special banquet [at] his private club, Dachshund let Kalambayi alert The Lodge to the survival of a baby dinosaur ('Bembe), knowing it would bring Prufrock to him. Prufrock led a team of operatives including Elvis Chestnut, Ginger Brown and Autumn Song to the Congo, where Dachshund's hunters managed to capture Prufrock. Autumn also captured the Dover Demon from The Lod[ge] for Dachshund's feast. However, Ginger and Elvis rescued 'Bembe and mounted an attack on Dachshund['s] club, during which Prufrock escaped. Prufrock broke Dachshund's left leg and returned with him to The Lod[ge]. Lodge director Leander Wight placed Dachshund and his hunters in a house on The Lodge's preserve located [in] the vicinity of the Fairies, a carnivorous species of miniature flying creatures. With a ring of iron surround-ing the house to ward the Fairies off, Dachshund and h[is] men would be safe from the Fairies only as long as the[y] remained on the premises.

As Dachshund's leg healed, he and his men made an alliance of convenience with a Chupacabra living on th[e] habitat, on the condition that they eventually help it kill Prufrock and all of his friends. The Chupacabra suppli[ed] Dachshund with an iron nail, but one of hunters used it in an escape attempt, only to be consumed by the Fairies. As the forces of the Cryptid supremacist Mi-Chen-Po began to assail The Lodge, Dachshund and some of his men finally escaped their prison by eating the Fairies one at a time.

AUTUMN SONG

ACKGROUND: Autumn Song is the great-anddaughter of a man who provided undisclosed to the Bigfoot John "Proof" Prufrock, risking his in the process. To pay his debt to the man's nily, Proof sold his remains to the family in vance, unaware his lifespan would greatly exceed other 100 years. Perhaps because of Proof's ability to fulfill his bargain to her family, Autumn s an intense loathing for all Cryptozoological eatures such as Proof ("Cryptids"). In recent years, tumn became an agent of The Lodge, a joint A-Canada organization established to liaise with yptids while offering a complete habitat on their ounds where the creatures could live in peace. tumn hoped to obtain a field assignment for The dge, but instead was assigned to the habitat. king advantage of her resources, Autumn began cretly capturing Cryptids and removing them her apartment where she could torture them death. Several fairies and gnomes numbered nongst her victims along with a Thunderbird; e also attempted to kill an Andean Wolf.

tumn made contact with Colonel Werner Dachs-nd, an enemy of The Lodge who fed upon Cryp-s. Autumn helped maneuver The Lodge into vestigating Dachshund's operation in the Demo-atic Republic of the Congo, intending to deliver oof to Dachshund. Autumn also kidnapped the ophesying Cryptid The Dover Demon for chshund's followers, but Proof escaped Autumn d Dachshund's trap, freed the Dover Demon and ptured Dachshund.

tumn fled capture and journeyed to Tibet, search-g the Himalayas for Zhen Ying, home of Mi-en-Po, Proof's adoptive brother. Autumn proposed alliance with Mi-Chen-Po and quickly recruited arc Ravello (ex-boyfriend of Proof's partner nger Brown) as one of their assistants. When oof went to Autumn's brother River to obtain aid in alyzing a severed finger believed to originate om one of Proof's long-lost relations, River manded Proof complete the bargain he made with s great-grandfather. However, Autumn intervened, ent on killing Proof before her brother could, nultaneously dispatching Marc to attack both nger Brown and Proof's girlfriend Isabella Bay. though supported by Mi-Chen-Po's Mongolian eath Worms, Autumn was defeated by Proof.

Y MICHAEL HOSKIN ART: RILEY ROSSMO

LEGAL NAME: Autumn Song
OTHER NAMES: None
OCCUPATION: Criminal operative, former federal agent
NATIONALITY: USA
LEGAL STATUS: Wanted in USA
BIRTHPLACE: Unrevealed
RELATIVES: Rain Song (brother), unidentified father and great-grandfather
MARITAL STATUS: Married
MEMBERSHIP: Formerly The Lodge
RESIDENCE: Zhen Ying, Tibet
EXTENT OF EDUCATION: Unrevealed
FIRST APPEARANCE: *Proof* #5 (February, 2008)

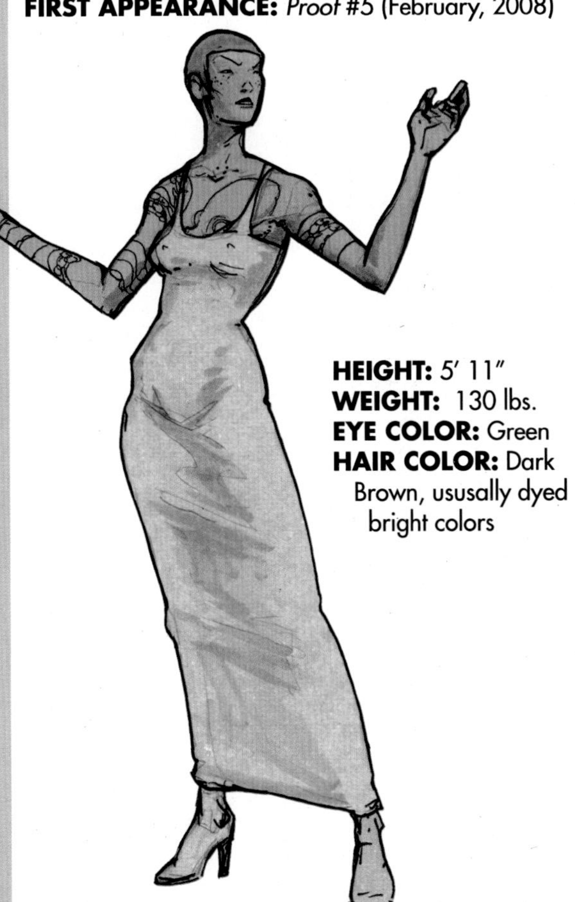

HEIGHT: 5' 11"
WEIGHT: 130 lbs.
EYE COLOR: Green
HAIR COLOR: Dark Brown, ususally dyed bright colors

CAPABILITIES: Autumn Song is an adept hand-to-hand combatant, marksman and knife wielder.

PARAPHERNALIA: Autumn usually carries a revolver and concealed knife. Since her affiliation with Mi-Chen-Po, she is often accompanied by an entourage of Cryptids.

CHUPACABRAS

FIRST APPEARANCE: *Proof* #1 (October, 2007)

The Chupacabra (also "Goatsucker," "Mexican Bigfoot," "Moca Vampire") is a family of cryptozoological creatures ("Cryptid") whose existence is unknown to the world at large. Chupacabra have thick, dark fur cover ing their bodies, doubtlessly inspiring their nickname "Mexican Bigfoot," despite having no apparent ties to the Bigfoot. Found primarily in Puerto Rico and Mexico, Chupacabra traditionally feed upon herding animals such as cattle, but will also consume humans, tunneling inside their victims to devour them from within. Chupacabra are careful to preserve the exterior of their victims so they can don the skin and masquerade as the victim whil seeking new prey. The Chupacabra's fur secretes chemicals which soak into the victim's skin, rendering it highly durable and resistant to weather and decay. Although Chupacabras normally speak in deep, raspy voices, wit practice they can imitate human speech.

At some point in recent years, a Chupacabra took possession of Leander Wight, director of The Lodge, a US-Canadian organization which liaises between humans and Cryptids, offering a habitat upon their grounds in Washington. "Leander" maintained his façade for some time, evidently either keeping his appetite under contr or concealing his victims.

At the same time, a Chupacabra from Mexico was enlisted by the Yeti Mi-Chen-Po to manip late his adoptive brother John "Proof" Prufroc a Bigfoot. Shortly after slaying and assuming the skin of a Mexican woman named Maria, Chupacabra was directed to journey to Seattl Washington and draw Proof to her. However, "Maria's" poor grasp of English led her to be misdirected to Minnesota, where she began working at Kennedy Meats meat packing plar After learning some English from her co-work Jeff (and killing most of the plant's staff after J was killed in a knife fight with another co-worker), "Maria" escaped into the Kekekabic Trail and took up residence in a cave, killing local passersby in the hopes of bringing Proof her.

fter killing and adopting the skin of hiker anette Levy, the Chupacabra journeyed to eward, Minnesota and the sheriff's office of vis Chestnut, unaware that Proof and his artner Ginger Brown had been alerted to anette's disappearance and were finally vestigating. In short order, the Chupacabra ew and skinned Nancy, a paramedic, llowed by Elvis's mother, Nadine. The hupacabra kept Nany's partner alive, tending to offer him to Proof as food, but hen Proof arrived he refused her. Although adine informed Proof that Mi-Chen-Po was aiting to rejoin him, Proof knew his brother y the name "Gilgamesh" and didn't under- and "Nadine's" message.

Nadine" was taken into Lodge custody and aced on the Habitat, while Elvis became a odge operative. "Nadine" maintained a rotesque fascination with Elvis, still claiming be his mother. Evidently feeling genuine aternal urges, "Nadine" adopted a trio of fant fairies, dubbing the boy Joy and twin rls Aranea and Nellie. "Nadine" would feed oon the fairies' blood, which actually helped e children combat their hereditary hemo- romatosis. Finding the Cryptid-eating olonel Dachshund and his men were also nprisoned on the Habitat, reined in by the esh-eating fairies which surrounded their ome, "Nadine" smuggled an iron nail to achshund, knowing the iron would ward off iries. One of Dachshund's men used the nail an escape attempt, only to quickly lose the bject and be devoured by the fairies, just as Nadine" had arranged.

Leander's" position became untenable when e US government learned he had misappro- riated funds and sent C.K. Dexter Haven to ssume control of The Lodge. With the real eander's wife Gloria having reappeared with e intent of exposing him, "Leander" shed his in and destroyed it, taking on the skin of odge employee Wayne Russet instead and ereby retaining control of The Lodge as Wayne," working with Haven. "Nadine" was oon made a field agent of The Lodge, part- ered with agent Belinda Drake in investigat- g Cryptid-related sightings. Meanwhile, Mi-Chen-Po had recruited a third Chupacabra nd had it don the skin of a US government gent to wrest control of the Lodge from Wayne." It remains unclear whether any of e three Chupacabras (save "Nadine") are ware of each other's true natures.

Y MICHAEL HOSKIN
RT: RILEY ROSSMO,
ELLY TINDALL & CHRIS GRINE

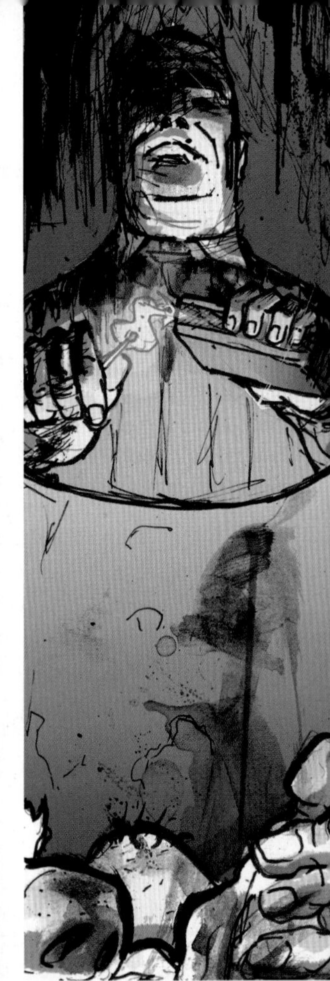

Mi-Chen-Po

BACKGROUND: A member of the Cryptozoological species ("Cryptid") called Yeti and named Gilgamesh by the "Gentleman Giant" Robert Winstone, owner of the Swift Brothers Circus, Gilgamesh accepted Winstone as his father and fellow attraction Gulliver (a Sasquatch, closely related to the Yeti) as his brother. Gilgamesh and Gulliver served as attractions in the circus together, but while Gulliver identified with the humans who patronized them, Gilgamesh became embittered by human culture, caring only for Winstone. Gilgamesh's feelings of isolation were only exacerbated by the fact he and Gulliver were the only representatives of their species either one knew.

While touring London, England in 1859, Gulliver and Gilgamesh became involved in the hunt for the killer Springheel Jack, who proved to be a pair of creatures committing brutal murders. During the investigation, Gulliver grew smitten with Julia Pastrana, a human woman whose hairy complexion was similar to a Sasquatch, but was in a loveless marriage with Thomas Lent. After Winstone died of a heart ailment, Gilgamesh lost any reason to continue associating peacefully with humans, but continued to support Gulliver. After Julia and her infant child's bodies were taxidermied and put on display by Lent, Gilgamesh obtained revenge on Gulliver's behalf through torturing Lent on an intestinal crank and taxidermied his body while Lent was still alive. After this, Gulliver and Gilgamesh went their separate ways, having grown too far apart emotionally.

Gilgamesh returned to Tibet and took up the name Mi-Chen-Po, residing within the temple of Zhen Ying in the Himalayas. Over time, Mi-Chen-Po amassed a small army of Cryptids, including Mongolian Death Worms, Bargests ("Devil Dogs") and at least one Chupacabra. By the 1970s Gulliver had become John Prufrock and served in The Lodge, an organization dedicated to assisting Cryptids and providing a preserve for them to live on. Recently, Mi-Chen-Po awakened the long-slumbering Golem Joseph Loew, hoping to recruit him into his army, but Loew refused to be Mi-Chen-Po's pawn. While searching for Loew, Prufrock's partner Ginger Brown encountered Mi-Chen-Po, who placed an unrevealed hypnotic suggestion into her mind.

When former Lodge agent Autumn Song quit the organization she sought out Mi-Chen-Po, who began allocating resources from his Cryptid army to assist her in attacks on Prufrock. Soon, Mi-Chen-Po himself set out personally to confront Prufrock while his and Autumn's forces prepared to unleash havoc on the Lodge's grounds.

LEGAL NAME: Mi-Chen-Po
OTHER NAMES: Gilgamesh, "Gilly"
OCCUPATION: Lord of Zhen Ying; former circus performer
NATIONALITY: None
LEGAL STATUS: No criminal record
BIRTHPLACE: Tibet
RELATIVES: Robert Winstone (adopted father, deceased), John Prufrock (adopted brother)
MARITAL STATUS: Unmarried
MEMBERSHIP: Formerly Swift Brothers Circus
RESIDENCE: Zhen Ying, Tibet
EXTENT OF EDUCATION: Unrevealed
FIRST APPEARANCE: *Proof* #13 (October, 2008)

HEIGHT: 7'2"
WEIGHT: 800 lbs.
EYE COLOR: Red
HAIR/FUR COLOR: White

CAPABILITIES: Mi-Chen-Po has exceptional superhuman strength and can heal wounds which would be fatal to humans. He has an unrevealed degree of skill in hypnosis, a sadistic understanding of torture and speaks both English and Mandarin.

PARAPHERNALIA: Mi-Chen-Po usually wields a wooden staff decorated with Thomas Lent's skull.

BY MICHAEL HOSKIN ART: RILEY ROSSMO